T0210008

Little Me, BIG Confessions

SHARIKA S. GERRICK

WestBow Press books may be ordered through booksellers or by contacting:

WestBow Press
A Division of Thomas Nelson & Zondervan
1663 Liberty Drive
Bloomington, IN 47403
www.westbowpress.com
844-714-3454

Because of the dynamic nature of the Internet, any web addresses or links contained in this book may have changed since publication and may no longer be valid. The views expressed in this work are solely those of the author and do not necessarily reflect the views of the publisher, and the publisher hereby disclaims any responsibility for them.

Any people depicted in stock imagery provided by Getty Images are models, and such images are being used for illustrative purposes only.
Certain stock imagery © Getty Images.

Scripture quotations marked (AMPC) taken from the Amplified® Bible (AMPC), Copyright © 1954, 1958, 1962, 1964, 1965, 1987 by The Lockman Foundation Used by permission. www.lockman.org

Scripture marked (KJV) taken from the King James Version of the Bible.

Scripture quotations marked MSG are taken from THE MESSAGE, copyright © 1993, 2002, 2018 by Eugene H. Peterson. Used by permission of NavPress, represented by Tyndale House Publishers. All rights reserved.

Scripture quotations marked (NIV) are taken from the Holy Bible, New International Version®, NIV®. Copyright © 1973, 1978, 1984, 2011 by Biblica, Inc.® Used by permission of Zondervan. All rights reserved worldwide. www.zondervan.com The "NIV" and "New International Version" are trademarks registered in the United States Patent and Trademark Office by Biblica, Inc.®

Scripture quotations marked (NLT) are taken from the Holy Bible, New Living Translation, copyright ©1996, 2004, 2015 by Tyndale House Foundation. Used by permission of Tyndale House Publishers, Carol Stream, Illinois 60188. All rights reserved.

ISBN: 978-1-6642-1919-9 (sc)
ISBN: 978-1-6642-1920-5 (e)

Library of Congress Control Number: 2021900422

Print information available on the last page.

WestBow Press rev. date: 03/16/2021

WESTBOW
PRESS®
A DIVISION OF THOMAS NELSON
& ZONDERVAN

But Jesus said, "Let the children come to me. Don't stop them! For the Kingdom of Heaven belongs to those who are like these children." And he placed his hands on their heads and blessed them before he left.

—Matthew 9:14–15 (New Living Translation)

This is my very first book, and I dedicate it to God. I thank Him for the gift to write. I thank Him for Jesus and the Holy Spirit. I thank Him for loving me and changing my life.

I would like to honor my Mom, Mozel Chisolm; and my Dad, the late Willie Gerrick Jr. who is now with the Great Cloud of Witnesses. God knew that you would be my parents and that I would go on to do great things and that you would be proud of me. I love you.

I would also like to honor my Spiritual Parents, Senior Pastor Kevin S. Rogers and First Lady Verndella Rogers. Thanks for your prayers, your love, your kindness, your wisdom, and your obedience when it comes to me. Thanks for speaking life into my life. I love you.

I honor my Grandparents, Willie Gerrick Sr. and the late Annie Mae Gerrick, and my grandmother Janie Sue Jones. I love you.

To my cousin Carlette Henry thanks for being there. I love you.

I am accepted in the beloved.

God loves me with an everlasting love!

God told them, "I've never quit loving you and never will. Expect love, love, and more love!" (Jeremiah 31:3 The Message)

To the praise of the glory of his grace, wherein he hath made us accepted in the beloved. (Ephesians 1:6)

The Lord hath appeared of old unto me, saying, Yea, I have loved thee with an everlasting love: therefore with lovingkindness have I drawn thee. (Jeremiah 31:3)

I am forgiving. I forgive as quickly and completely as the Master forgave me.

Forgive as quickly and completely as the Master forgave you. (Colossians 3:13 MSG)

I am patient, and I am kind.

Love endures long and is patient and kind.
(1 Corinthians 13:4 The Amplified Bible, Classic
Edition)

For God hath not given us the spirit of fear; but of power, and of love, and of a sound mind. (2 Timothy 1:7)

And he arose, and rebuked the wind, and said unto the sea, Peace, be still. And the wind ceased, and there was a great calm. (Mark 4:39)

I can do all things through Christ,
who strengthens me. I am the
righteousness of God in Christ
Jesus, and I am as bold as a lion.

2 Corinthians 5:21 (NLT)

For God made Christ, who never sinned to be the offering for our sin, so that we could be made right with God through Christ Jesus

I can do all things through Christ which strengtheneth me. (Philippians 4:13)

The wicked flee when no man pursueth: but the righteous are bold as a lion. (Proverbs 28:1)

stomach virus

cancer

fever

adhd

cold(a cold)

mental retardation

influenza

sickle cell

mental illness

throat cancer

stomach cancer

By Jesus's stripes, I am healed.

But he was wounded for our transgressions, he was bruised for our iniquities: the chastisement of our peace was upon him; and with his stripes we are healed. (Isaiah 53:5)

I am well favoured of the Lord. There is a spirit of intelligence in me.

Children in whom was no blemish, but well favoured, and skillful in all wisdom, and cunning in knowledge, and understanding science, and such as had ability in them to stand in the king's palace, and whom they might teach the learning and the tongue of the Chaldeans. (Daniel 1:4)

But there is [a vital force] a spirit [of intelligence] in man, and the breath of the Almighty gives men understanding. (Job 32:8 AMPC)

God's word is life, and it is
true. I speak life only.

Death and life are in the power of the tongue:
and they that love it shall eat the fruit thereof.
(Proverbs 18:21)

Then said Jesus to those Jews which believed on
him, If ye continue in my word, then are ye my
disciples indeed; And ye shall know the truth, and
the truth shall make you free. (John 8:31–32)

I concentrate on doing my best for God. I study God's word of truth, and I study for my classes to improve and make good grades.

Concentrate on doing your best for God, work you won't be ashamed of, laying out the truth plain and simple. (2 Timothy 2:15 MSG)

I am created in the image of God, and I have dominion! Jesus already defeated Satan, and he is under my feet!

And God said, Let us make man in our image, after our likeness: and let them have dominion over the fish of the sea, and over the fowl of the air, and over the cattle, and over all the earth, and over every creeping thing that creepeth upon the earth. So God created man in his own image, in the image of God created he him; male and female created he them. (Genesis 1:26–27)

I obey my spiritual parents, and I honour my mom and dad, for this is right and the *First* Commandment with promise. I work at obeying them in and out of their presence.

Children, obey your parents in the Lord: for this is right. Honour thy father and mother; which is the first commandment with promise; That it may be well with thee, and thou mayest live long on the earth. (Ephesians 6:1-3)

I *am* fearfully and wonderfully made (beautiful/handsome) inside and out.

I will praise thee; for I am fearfully and wonderfully made: marvellous are thy works; and that my soul knoweth right well. (Psalm 139:14)

I am the blessed of the Lord. I give,
and it shall be given unto me.

Give, and it shall be given unto you; good measure, pressed down, and shaken together, and running over shall men give into your bosom. For with the same measure that ye mete withal it shall be measured to you again. (Luke 6:38)

The blessing of the Lord—it makes [truly] rich, and He adds no sorrow with it [neither does toiling increase it]. (Proverbs 10:22 AMPC)

I am blessed. By faith, my life,
Church, home, school, health, family,
godly relationships, assignment,
and finances are blessed.

Blessed shalt thou be when thou comest in,
and blessed shalt thou be when thou goest out.
(Deuteronomy 28:6)

I am an overcomer by the
blood of the Lamb and by the
word of my testimony!

And they overcame him by the blood of the Lamb,
and by the word of their testimony; and they loved
not their lives unto the death. (Revelation 12:11)

I read, study, and meditate (think on, speak, and say) God's Word daily. His Word is my number 1 priority.

But seek ye first the kingdom of God, and his righteousness; and all these things shall be added unto you. (Matthew 6:33)

This book of the law shall not depart out of thy mouth; but thou shalt meditate therein day and night, that thou mayest observe to do according to all that is written therein: for then thou shalt make thy way prosperous, and then thou shalt have good success. (Joshua 1:8)

God's thoughts toward me

are peace and not evil, to give

me an expected end!

For I know the thoughts that I think toward you,

saith the Lord, thoughts of peace, and not of evil,

to give you an expected end. (Jeremiah 29:11)

About the Author

Sharika Gerrick is a devoted Christian. She grew up in a small town called Blackville, S.C. At age 18 years old, she joined the military months before graduating from High School. She served on active duty in the U.S. Army for a little over 6 years and then finished the remainder of her time in the IRR. It was during her time as a Soldier where God lead Sharika to the Church where she is a member in Washington State and she truly gave her life to Christ and got re-baptized. Since that time, things have never been the same. She has seen the change, the growth, and the progress not only within herself but, in her life by sitting under the word, learning to believe God's word of truth, and learning to live and walk by faith. Not only has she seen the change in her life but, progress in her family. She knows without a doubt that God changed her.

Sharika is a college graduate. She graduated from American Public University System with her Bachelor of Arts Degree in Management with a Concentration in Human Resources Management. She is currently a graduate student at American Public University System. She will soon be a second time graduate from American Public University System with her Masters Degree in Management with a Concentration in Strategic Consulting.

She gives God the glory for the gift of writing. She has a seer to guider her. She now has the anointing. The anointing to see clearly, the anointing to write, and clarity. Sharika prays that this book is a blessing to all who read it. God bless you now and forever more.

Printed in the United States
by Baker & Taylor Publisher Services